THE LIMERICK BIBLE

100 Biblical Limericks

John M. Scott

Fairway Press
Lima, Ohio

THE LIMERICK BIBLE

FIRST EDITION
Copyright © 1995
John M. Scott

ISBN 1-55673-983-4

To: my unnamed ancient Celtic ancestor who inspired this legend:

"If you spend the night on Snowden Mountain, alone, by the time morning comes, you will either be dead, mad, or a poet."

Table Of Contents

WARNINGS

A BIBLICAL WARNING
"Only take heed, and keep your soul diligently, lest you forget the things which your eyes have seen, and lest they depart from your heart all the days of your life; make them known to your children and your children's children — — Deuteronomy 4:9

> If we forget where we've been we can blow it,
> And who we are, we can keep, or forego it.
> Without the bible you see,
> We could easily be,
> Walkin' through God's home town and not know it.

A PARTIARCHAL WARNING ostensibly from St.Edward (Lear) 1812-1888
When buying a book of limericks, be extremely "Leary".

A WARNING ABOUT THE AUTHOR
John M. Scott is a working parish pastor in the Western Pennsylvania Conference of the United Methodist Church, a storyteller, and limrist. He is a man who has Pete Seeger's autograph; has spoken directly to Garrison Keillior's secretary; and has visited the cave where another patron saint, Jerome, translated The Vulgate. His life project is translating the bible (and some Church Fathers) into limerick form.

FOREWORD

The Limerick Bible is a "side dish" on your theological banquet table. This is not the main course. Accompanying the full meal they add their flavor to the feast. Limericks may also be served alone, as "snacks", but don't overdo. Like Proverbs and cheese blintzes, one at a time is best. The "main course" is the biblical message, prepared according to your own recipe, and ingredients of study, evaluation, interpretation, and understanding. This may take the form of lesson, lecture, sermon, opening devotion, speech, report, or simply sharing around a discussion circle.

This book asks: Could a limerick help? Here you will find careful bible study, reduced to a thesis sentence, and then expanded to five lines, AABBA, the limerick form. Thus, you might serve one of these alongside everything else, or just pop one into your mouth for its own sake. Receive them as a gift. If you like the taste, try the recipe yourself.

Consider:

Limericks are "read-able": they don't ask for much time.

Limericks are "remember-able": they can help you remember the biblical who's who, and what's what.

Limericks are "remark-able": They can highlight a point or teaching you wish to emphasize.

However: they do have a reputation...

> The limerick is frequently crude.
> Often common, bawdy, or rude.
> This genre's no sonnet
> With lace tied upon it,
> But anatomical, vile, and/or lewd.

> Would the Word descend down-to-earth
> To make use of such five lines of verse?

The limerick, complete
From head to clay feet
Seems a genre of questionable worth.

Yet Bible uses slaves, maidens, an impotent clerk,
The bereft, the barren, an occasional jerk.
God often chooses,
The tools that he uses,
From those deemed least likely to work.

So if one of these limericks graces you with pleasure, adds
a flavorful insight to your theological banquet, or makes the
bible more read-able, remark-able, remember-able, then a purpose
has been served, a hope realized, and this endeavor justified.

A final thought: This is a book that relates to the bible,
thus you might like to purchase it for someone else. Rumor has
it that this is the primary motivating force in bible sales.

JMS

GENESIS 1-11   Overture To A Storyteller's Notebook

Genesis 1-11: Primitive stories? No, just longstanding. They represent the storyteller's art in a sophisticated oral culture of the past. Here is the oldest existing set of notes for a storytelling session. They come at the beginning of the bible. They are an overture. They set the stage for the drama to come.

I. THE OVERTURE   Genesis 1:26-3:22 in limerick form
...then the Lord God formed man of dust from the ground...
Genesis 2:7

The Creation saga in five lines:

As human we are almost like gods.
But, the "almost" makes ominous odds.
Given power to destroy, we
Can screw things up royally.
A dangerous position for clods.

II. CREATION: A Twice Told Tale Genesis 1:1-2:4a and 2:4b-25

Creation stories are not one, but two.
In your pocket carry both to review.
Each is a must,
One says, "Thou art dust."
The other, "This universe, I made for you."

The rabbis would say: In my pocket I carry two stones. From time to time I pull out a stone and read what is written upon it. On one is written: "Thou art dust", and on the other: "The universe is made for you." I need both stones.

III. ADAM AND EVE.   Genesis 2

Genesis 2:22-23 ...and the rib which the Lord God had taken from the man he made into a woman and brought her to the man. Then the man said, "This at last is bone of my bones and flesh of my flesh; she shall be called Woman, because she was taken out of Man."

The Hebrew language is concrete. Words point to the tangible. We do not find abstractions like: "soul", instead we find the corporeal, the physical: "bones"

Boy Meets Girl   Genesis 2:22-23

"Bone of my bones," was Adam's decree.
Concrete term, no abstract thinker, he.
Were he romantic instead,
He might rather have said:
"When I look within you, I find me!".

Eden and Points East   Genesis 3:7-10
Then the eyes of both were opened, and they knew that they were naked; and they sewed fig leaves together and made themselves aprons. ("naked" as in "defenseless", -they were caught.)

Back in Eden the two came to grief.
Defenseless in their naked belief...
They made excuses to God
Who thought it was odd
The uses they found for a leaf.

...therefore the Lord God sent him forth from the garden of Eden, to till the ground from which he was taken.

Outside Eden they found still more grief.
With no hope for return or relief.
But they weren't left forlorn,
Cain and Able were born.
Had Adam overturned a new leaf?

IV. THE CHILDREN OF ADAM
Cain and Abel   Genesis 4:4-7

...and Abel brought of the firstlings of his flock and of their fat portions. And the Lord had regard for Abel and his offering, but for Cain and his offering he had no regard. So Cain was very angry, and his countenance fell. The Lord said to Cain,... If you do well, will you not be accepted?

Cain   Genesis 4:1-7

Cain and Abel planned a Thanksgiving stew,
A cover-dish meal for the God that each knew.
Abel brought out his best,
But Cain failed the test,
When he said, "Any old thing to make do."

and Abel   Genesis 4:4

The message seems very clear.
God says to us "Do not fear,
Just do your best,
And then let it rest,
'My regards' are the words that you'll hear."

The Flood   Genesis 8:11

...and the dove came back to him in the evening and low, in her
mouth a freshly plucked olive leaf;....

> The Divine tried right-handed power.
> And sent forth a world-record shower.
> With it all down the drain,
> God said, "Never again."
> Noah's dove came back with a flower.

The City of Babel   Genesis 11:1+

 Now the whole earth had one language <u>and few words</u>... in the
land of Shinar... they said... let us make bricks...

> See Shem. See Shem build.
> Build Shem. Build and gild.
> Shinar is finer,
> Even diviner.
> We God. We big. We skilled.

V. THE OVERTURE'S OVER

"Oh Abram..."   Blessed to be a blessing

"Now the Lord said to Abram, 'Go..'." opening words of Genesis 12

The overture's over; the stage is now set.
The background completed, the drama is yet.
But no floods, nor confusion,
In God's way he's now choose'n,
Says to Abram, "Now go, I've blessings to let.".

PEOPLE b.c.e. Dramatis Personae

Open the bible and out come characters: -a man with two sons, a king, a queen, and a prophet; another man with two sons, a talking snake; a mule with a message, prophets, disciples, judges, and the judged. Characters.

I. FOUR FATHERS

There are limits. There are norms. There are rules. There are standards. And then there are times the Divine wishes to make a point.

Abram   Genesis 18:12+

So Sarah laughed to herself,... The Lord said to Abraham, "Why did Sarah laugh, and say, 'Shall I indeed bear a child, now that I am old?' Is anything too hard for the Lord?

> A curious quirk in God's style,
> Whose ways often charm and beguile.
> For the Father of Nations,
> Chose a man whose relations
> With his wife, fathered only a smile.

Methuselah   Genesis 5:26-27

Methuselah lived after the birth of Lamech seven hundred and eighty-two years, and had other sons and daughters. Thus all the days of Methuselah were nine hundred and sixty-nine years; and he died.

George Gershwin Ain't Necessarily So
>   (may be sung to the tune, as in Porgy & Bess)
> Methuselah lived nine hundred years,
> Methuselah lived nine hundred years,
> Well actually the score,
> Claims sixty-nine more,
> And children unnumbered - who hears?

Noah   Genesis 5:32
After Noah was five hundred years old, Noah became the father
of Shem, Ham, and Japheth.

We know Noah's boat best, 'cause his crew
Kept Creation afloat like a zoo.
He got that crew, so they say
When in the biblical way,
Thrice anew Mrs. Noah, Noah knew.

Israel (Jacob)   Genesis 37:3
Now Israel loved Joseph more than any other of his children,
because he was the son of his old age;...

These four fathers of Genesis knew
Their wives when at plus 62,
They were heard to say, "Whee,
This beats the AARP,
And sitting around with nothing to do.

II. CHOSEN PEOPLE

"Sometime, ... could you choose someone else?"
                              Tevia in "Fiddler on the Roof"

Jubal   Genesis 4:21
...he was the father of all those who play the lyre and pipe.

"Have you invented instruments new and bazaar?"
Asked Jubal's dad expecting maybe, "guitar?".
But the kid so forlorn,
Holding up a ram's horn,
Said, "This is all I've come up with, shofar!"

Melchizedek   Genesis 14:18 (and Psalm 110:4; Hebrews 5,6)
          -with an Irish brogue

Ah sure Melchizedek is a grand old name.
For his job he made no ancestral claim.
Name your child from this verse
And you could do worse,
Genesis-Psalms-Hebrews, his priesthood proclaim.

Joseph   Genesis 50:20
    ...you meant evil against me; but God meant it for good...

His brothers sold Joseph, decreeing
The end of those dreams he was seeing.
But the deed to prevent,
The dream's full intent,
Is the very thing that brought it to being.

Pharaoh   Exodus 5:2

When Moses gave Pharaoh a "nix",
Pharaoh said, "That, me off, it sure ticks.
O Moses my pigeon,
You should stick to "religion",
And keep your nose out of my politics.

Rahab   Joshua 6:25
        may be sung to the tune: "House Of The Rising Sun"

But Rahab the harlot, and her father's household, and all who
belonged to her, Joshua saved alive; and she dwelt in Israel to
this day, because she hid the messengers whom Joshua sent to
spy out Jericho.
(Note: a "billet" is lodging for a soldier, especially in
nonmilitary or public buildings)

There is a house in Jericho, where the door stays open late.
So when Josh sent spies into the town, inside the city gate,
He said, "If it's tough,
And spying gets rough, (inside the city gate)
When the coast is clear, just drop in here and Rahab-bilitate

Goliath   I Samuel 17:4

There was a big man from Gath,
Stood in the valley venting his wrath.
To God's People he called,
"Yahweh's toothless and bald!"
David said, "I'll head him off in the pass."

David   In Saul's Armor   I Samuel 17:38-39
Then Saul clothed David with his armor; he put a helmet of
bronze on his head, and clothed him with a coat of mail. And
David girded his sword over his armor, and he tried in vain to go,
for he was not used to them. Then David said to Saul, "I cannot
go with these; for I am not used to them." And David put them
off.

If you live long enough you will find,
A new generation comes up behind.
With a gleam in their eye
Their own armor to try,
Tools of the past often pinch, or they bind.

The Queen of Sheba   or: "Sheba, The Movie"   I Kings 10:1-3

Hollywood would have loved such a plot.
Sheba's Queen came and brought quite a lot.
But as Sol answered questions,
Wisdom fathered suggestions.
In a movie that's no tickets bought.

Jezebel   1 Kings 16:31-33

She was the queen that shared Ahab's throne.
This first lady from Sidon it's known,
Just wanted to share,
The religion from there,
But the Jews already had one of their own.

Ahab   1 Kings 22:39

Israel's Captain, Ahab of old,
Like Melville's Ahab we're told,
Had a penchant for white,
Thought that ivory might,
For a palace be better than gold.

Nebuchadnezzar   Daniel 4:28-37

Old Nebu ate grass like an ox,
And his hair grew long curly locks,
And all from this thing
Of who really is King!
But with priorities straight now he walks.

III. PROPHETS

In all of time's speech and literature, there is none to compare.

Jonah   Prophets As Cathartic (Purging) Jonah 1:15-16
    Jonah 1:2 "Arise, go to Nineveh, that great city, and cry
      against it; for their wickedness has come up before me."

    Old Jonah was told all along
    "Go to Nineveh and sing 'em your song".
    For those not believ'n
    He proved that not even
    Can a whale stomach prophets for long.

Habakkuk   Habakkuk 2:4b, 3:17-18
    Habakkuk 2:4b: ...but the righteous shall live by his faith.

   Easy For You To Say-
    We look at such things* as polemic,
    Problematic, or just academic.
    But try a walk-through
    Should such happen to you,
    "The just shall live by faith" now systemic.

    * Though the fig tree do not blossom, nor fruit be on the
    vines, the produce of the olive fail and the fields yield no
    food, the flock be cut off from the fold and there be no
    herd in the stalls, yet I will rejoice in the Lord, I will
    joy in the God of my salvation.

Elijah   the Prophet, Nabi   1 Kings 19:12
      (A prophet's Hebrew title, pronounced: naw-be')

Elijah the prophet, nabi,
Fled to a cave, the Lord, there to see.
But the Word to inspire,
Came not in earth, wind, or fire,
But a still small voice said, "It's Me!"

Elisha   -a scholarly report   2 Kings 2:23-25
Can a passage of scripture have more than one meaning? Consider this story as seen by a variety of scholars.

Elisha went up from there to Bethel; and while he was going up on the way, some small boys came out of the city and jeered at him, saying, "Go up, you baldhead! Go up, you baldhead!" And he turned around, and when he saw them, he cursed them in the name of the Lord. And two she-bears came out of the woods and tore forty-two of the boys. From there he went on to Mount Carmel, and thence he returned to Samaria.

First, as seen by students of: Redaction Criticism
    (finding the author's intent behind his words)

    In Elisha's story they included a verse in
    Where he calls two bears to chew on youth who were curse'n.
    What was the author's desire?
    Did he hope to inspire?
    Or simply endear us to the prophet as person!

Second, as seen by students of: Etiological Stories.
    (stories about the beginning of something)

    In Elisha's story they included a verse in
    Where he calls two bears to chew on youth who were curse'n.
    Their unbearable curse
    Underwent a reverse-
    The beginning of Pediatric Care Nursin'.

Third, as seen by students of: Form Criticism.
    (determining the nature of a text by its form.)

In Elisha's story they included a verse in
Where he calls two bears to chew on youth who were curse'n.
Well would you look there,
This thing is a prayer!
Supplication, the situation reversin'.

Fourth, as seen by students of: Source Criticism.
    (trying to understand the nature of a text by identifying
    its source.)

From whence did this story first come?
I think that the youth would play dumb.
My guess is Elisha for truth,
But did he count all those youth?
And the bears would inflate the sum.

Fifth: the pious, scholarly or not, seeking comfort in prayer.

The book's most unusual prayer,
Is said by a guy with no hair.
Later it's said,
God knows the hairs on your head,
And obviously, where to find bears.

PEOPLE a.d.

I.   FOUR GOOD SPELLS
II. SELECTED SAINTS
III. CHURCH FATHERS

I. FOUR GOOD SPELLS gospel= good + spell- (spell is an archaic word for "discourse, speaking". To sit and spell meant to sit and talk. A "Spell" is a spoken word, with power.)

Matthew

In order, Matthew's first of the four.
Builds on Mark, borrows Luke, adds his store.
His story just beams
With Exodus themes,
Out of Egypt comes a kingdom once more.

Mark

We think Mark heard Peter preaching God's glories,
And so wrote the first of these foremost good stories.
Be he the first one or not,
His story traveled a lot,
And cast a good spell on some world-class type worries.

Luke

Luke's work is a medicine divine.
It's a dose universal, sublime.
I think Luke takes his cue,
From a man he once knew,
Some guy named Paul with whom he traveled one time.

John

Before John wrote, he shuffled the deck.
A new order, an account circumspect.
In books of signs and of glory,
John chose parts of the story,
With the goal "your belief", he'd select.

II. SELECTED SAINTS

Joseph of Nazareth
Joseph, like Joseph his ancestor-old,
Was a dreamer, of dreams in which God foretold,
A coming agenda,
Wherein God would soon send ya,
To Egypt!, from whence would salvation unfold.

The Wise Men   Matthew 2:2
What was it that told them to "Go!" ?
That it's not enough just to know.
"He is born", the stars said,
But a deeper Voice led,
"Enough theory, you have gifts to bestow."

Nicodemus   John 3:4+
"Ole, Nicodemus," said Jesus, "Don't blow it.
This birth's when Spirit and water bestow it.
But without it you see,
You might easily be
Walkin' through God's hometown and not know it."

Among the 12   A Patron Saint for the Solitary Soul
Here's to Bar-thola-mew,
Gospel words about him so few.
We feel certain that Bart
Accomplished his part,
Just that Matthew et.al. never knew.

Saul of Tarsus   Acts 9:1-2
There once was a man from Tarsus,
Who said in a fit of catharsis,
"I will arrange
To put Christians in chains-
Disrespect for the Law makes me nauseous."

Paul of Tarsus   2 Corinthians 12:9
There once was a man quite deficient,
The thorn-in-his-side non-remissent,
Who thought for awhile,
And heard Someone smile-
"My grace for you is sufficient"

WHEN GOD SELECTS   5 limericks on Divine Call
1. The Promise
A curious quirk in God's style,
Whose ways often charm and beguile.
For the Father of Nations,
Chose a man whose relations
With his wife fathered only a smile.

2. The People
For a People to introduce Himself through,
It's quite strange God would choose the Hebrew.
Yet the God who would rule,
Picked some slaves! as His tool,
Just to show Who does what and to who.

3. The Place

Can anything good come from there?
Through a maid with no male for an heir?
Then an angel said, "Dear,
There is nothing to fear,
There's no dread in God's will or His care".

4. The Person

They were all looking high for a King.
Recalling David who taught 'em to sing.
The Messiah expected
Could not be rejected,
Who'd think a stable's birth-cry the thing?

5. The Pattern

A curious quirk, in a Strange Divine Planner
When calling forth leaders to carry His banner.
God seems always quite prone
The "least likely" to phone,
Including you, in some way, shape, or manner.

III. CHURCH FATHERS

Polycarp 70-156?   a bishop of Smyrna
    He was the gentlest and strongest of men,
    Submissive only to God, so that when,
    Lion and lamb
    Laid down in this man,
    The combination proved stronger than sin.

Origen   186-253   his hometown was Alexandria, Egypt
    Origen taught, studied, and wrote.
    The church's first scholar of note.
    His main lesson plan:
    God, close to Man,
    And not in some Kingdom remote.

Callistus I ?-222   a slave who became pope
    His love of forgiveness we're praising,
    Back then he knew grace was amazing.
    Surprisingly able
    To bring to God's table
    The sinner most vile or debasing.

Thomas Aquinas   1225-1274   loved the syllogism, thus...
    Jesus was a master teacher. / Jesus taught by telling stories.
      Therefore, the best way to teach is to tell stories.

    Summing everything up Thomas wrote
    In his Summa Theological Note:
    "The best way to teach is
    Tell a story, like Jesus."
    But, not one story does Tom tell or quote.

Augustine of Hippo   354-430
        author: The Confessions. The City of God.
The works of Augustine give evidence that the limerick form
would have been a useful tool in antiquity. Compare the prose
version with what Augustine the Limrist might have written.

The Augustinian Doxology, The Confessions. Book 1, Chapter 1

In prose form:
"Great art thou, O Lord, and greatly to be praised; great is thy
power, and thy wisdom infinite. And thee would man praise:
man, a part of thy creation; man, who bears about him his
mortality, the witness of his sins, even the witness that thou dost
resist the proud. Yet man would praise thee, he who is part of
thy creation. Thou awakest us to delight in praising thee; for
thou hast made us for thyself and our hearts are restless till they
find rest in thee."
        (Augustine, The Confessions. Book I, Chapter 1)

In limerick form:

        What is man that he should give praise?
        The created, who changes all ways.
        Mortal, yet proud,
        Who sins with the crowd,
        Still delights in his God all his days.

41

The text continues, wrestling with a basic theological decision.

In prose form:
"Grant then, Lord, that I may know and understand whether first to call upon thee or to praise thee; whether first to know thee or to call upon thee; But who can call upon thee, not knowing thee? For he that knoweth thee not may call on thee as other than thou art. Or, is it rather, that we call on thee that we may know thee? But how shall they call on him in whom they have not believed? Or how shall they believe without a preacher?"
   (Augustine, The Confessions. Book I, Chapter 1)

In limerick form:
   Which is first, that we know God at all?
   Or, first call when our back's to the wall?
   If introductions are needed
   Knowledge surely's impeded.
   That's why God gives to preachers a call.

Had Augustine used the limerick when he wrote The City of God...
   Readable, short, and sweet:
   Church Fathers for the man-in-the-street.
      One ponders alas,
      A Dark Ages bypass;
      Had The City of God been so neat.

PARABLES

PARABLE: The Lost: Sheep, Coins, Son   Luke 15

Luke 15:1-2: Now the tax collectors and sinners were all drawing near to hear him. And the Pharisees and the scribes murmured saying, "This man receives sinners and eats with them." So he told them... (3 parables).

The New Testament understanding of "carrying a cross" includes the "volunteer factor". When people refer to something inflicted upon them as "the cross I bear", they misunderstand the biblical phrase. You must volunteer for a cross. Luke 15 describes 3 persons who volunteer. In numbering the lost, the movement is from 100 to 10 to 1. But the movement in the plot is the same in each story: loss, voluntary search, joy. Picking up a cross is a volunteer venture.

A man with one hundred sheep,
A woman with ten coins in her keep,
A man with two boys,
Each found that the joys
Of modeling God made them weep.

They wept first with grief at their loss,
These three who now pick up a cross.
But, their stories have ends
In which they call upon friends,
And weep with joy at the parties they toss.

PARABLE: The Man With Two Sons   Luke 15:11-32

And he said, "There was a man who had two sons;..."

The parable in scripture form is open-ended. We are left to decide whether the Older Son came to the party. The limerick version suggests a possible solution.

The Man With Two Sons

We've named it, "The Prodigal Son,"
Cause we think it's about number one.
Named so by the church
Who stayed on the perch
But with "two sons" the story's begun.

On The One Hand

From the start we anticipate trouble,
With a son who's head is a bubble.
It's easy to spot
This turn in the plot,
So why the line-up to look like his double?

The Other Hand

As the older son leaned on his hoe.
The red from his neck gave a glow.
"In derision, I laugh...
Looks like me and the calf
Get the short end in this deal, don't ya know.

All I want is what I am due.
Just see it from my point of view...
I believe in hard work!
And Dad's a big jerk!
I've earned it, by God, now come through."

Epilogue   I Corinthians 13

There is one older son that I know,
That the biblical record can show,
Came in to the party;
Raised his glass with a hearty:
"Love is patient, and kind; don't aim low."

Make love your aim. -Paul in I Corinthians 14:1

PARABLE: The Good Samaritan   Luke 10:25-37
or
A Left/Right Brain Approach to Torah
or
The One About The Lawyer and the Storyteller

Luke 10:25-27:   And behold, a lawyer stood up to put him to the
test, saying, "Teacher, what shall I do to inherit eternal life?"
He said to him, "What is written in the law? How do you read?"
And he answered, "You shall love the Lord your God with all
your heart, and with all your soul, and with all your strength, and
with all your mind; and your neighbor as yourself."   And he
said to him, "You have answered right, do this, and you will
live." But he, desiring to justify himself, said to Jesus, "And
who is my neighbor?"
       There follows Jesus' story...
              -The Good Samaritan-
And Jesus said to him, "Go and do likewise."

 Luke, the gospel collector, was not familiar with theories of
Left/Right Brain Function, although, I find it represented in
chapter 10. This modern concept of a dual brain strikingly
describes human thought. It portrays a "left side" that is
logical, rational, and as quantative as 2x2. It says "Mary Brown
has flat feet."   Lawyers function here.
     But, the theory also describes a "right side" that functions
as analogic, (analogy, comparison, metaphor) imaginative, and as
qualitative as grace. Of Mary Brown it says, "She walks in
beauty like the night". Storytellers function here.

47

The Left/Right Brain Theory Of Luke 10:

A lawyer, typically left-brained
Choose a creed for the "Torah-explained."
But this other feller,
A short-story teller
Told a tale, and his words have remained.

It's a story of "life round the bend."
Where people pass by, or descend,
To the level of need
That transcends any creed,
And in truth, we decide on the end.

The first round the bend wore priest's clothes.
For the second, a Levite he chose.
A pattern reflected!
So third was expected:
A layman! But not one of those.

Conclusion
It hangs like the tale of a kite,
Dangling there, an imperative bite.
A compound of "go",
With "do likewise", and so:
The Torah, by the brain on the right.

"You shall love the Lord your God with all... your mind;"
-the Shema, quoted by an unnamed lawyer and Jesus of Nazareth.

THE LABORERS AND THE VINEYARD
Matthew 20:1-16

or

Judgementgrace

or

What the Kingdom of God is Like

or

The Mysterious Marvelous Vineyard Owner

or

A Long Story and A Short Question

The Story:

He's up at an ungodly hour.
With fear that his grapes may go sour,
So agreeing to pay,
A good wage for the day,
He sends workers to pick vine, and bower.

But the harvest is more than expected,
More than can be picked by the workers selected.
So at the 9 o'clock call,
It's get back to the Hall
And hire those beforehand rejected.

He goes again at noon and at three,
Makes a deal, non-specific, you see.
"I'm good for my word,
As you have probably heard.
I'll make it right, just come work for me."

Now, darkness will fall in one hour,
Still time to find a few more to hire,
His choices now, though,
Are the lame, blind, and slow,
And generally, those with no power.

Pause to consider the contracts they've sealed,
As each crew arrives and enters the field.
The question first asked-
"What's the pay for this task?"
They want to know what their labors will yield.

So it's quite normal as they begin,
To calculate from the time they punch in.
The pay they expect
All quite correct
Is per diem over hour put in.

Now comes a most unusual ploy,
Perhaps born out of mischievous joy,
He calls his foreman to say,
"When you hand out the pay
Do it last-first, and first-last, Ho-boy!"

They had but one hour, to pick grapes for the wine,
And now there they stand, at the front of the line.
When they look at their pay,
The rest hear them say:
"A full day's wage, in your's and in mine!"

So now the excitement release.
Down the line goes the news of "Increase!".
If those bums get such pay,
Think what is due for "all day",
This guy owes a paycheck obese.

Now we get to the crux of our plot,
As we hear what the first-hired got.
They cannot disguise
Their total surprise
On receiving the exact deal they sought.

Now the grumbling noises begin,
As they commit unoriginal sin.
"I think we are due
More than the 5 o'clock crew,
Your decision on pay scale: rescind!"

Says the Owner, "Don't give me distress.
You agreed, and you got fair redress.
What I do with my own,
And the grace that I've shown
Seems a judgement on pride centered stress."

Commentary:

> They're together like strands in a rope,
> In this story of unconditional hope.
> It's both Judgement and Grace
> In a grand interface,
> Cuts and heals like Grandma's lye soap.

> God's grace is for raising "the dead".
> But we reward the rewardable instead.
> Then watch judgement fall,
> As we reject grace-for-all,
> If we can see it through the eyes in our head.

The Question:

"Is your eye evil, because I do good?" - a question in the bible
Matthew 20:15

ADDING TO SCRIPTURE: a suggested epilogue for the Church.
or,
"This Cup is My Blood"
Come back later, when the wine has been pressed,
And the Owner calls a festive taste-test.
Remembering the dream
Of his equal-pay scheme
Says, "It's good wine this year- just the best".

BIBLICAL BOOKS

(Genesis, the Prophets, and Gospels have their own chapters)

Genesis

> The Design was there from the start,
> Disobedience then played a part.
> But the story is still,
> Not over until
> We see again God's original art.

Exodus   A trip to the "Promised Land"-

> God's People took the "Road Out"
> And mosied around and about,
> But yet in all things,
> It's change that time brings,
> Now it's they who host pilgrims devout.

Ruth

> The Book of Ruth has an unusual plot.
> Good and Evil just don't fight a lot.
> Right from the beginning,
> Goodness is winning,
> Whither thou goest there's goodness begot.

Song of Solomon

Some say "This is not about sex.
It's a metaphor profound and complex."
But read it and see
If you don't agree,
The literal makes the most interesting text.

Job   I had heard of thee by the hearing of the ear, but now my
        eye sees thee;.... (42:5)

Job's story in summation quite terse,
May be found in 42, the fifth verse.
It's the shift in one's being,
From "hearing" to "seeing",
Next enter: Psalms! and your spirit immerse.

Psalms

Choose the words of a Psalm when you pray.
God's own word to man, by the way.
God's Word going out,
Is turned round about,
So that God gets an instant replay.

Proverbs

The proverbs are not meant to rhyme-
Though they're short, read one at a time.
Changing so fast that it tickles,
They move from dead men to pickles-
Subjects earthy, wise, and sublime.

Ecclesiastes (or The Speaker)   Ecclesiastes 1:2

"Emptiness of emptiness, says the Speaker, emptiness, All is
empty." -New English Bible translation (RSV translates:
"Vanity of vanities, says the Preacher,)
    Note also, there is no doctrine of the hereafter in
Ecclesiastes' mind. Thus...

Two Poets, Two Views: Robert Browning replies to Ecclesiastes

Mamma said, they'd be days like this, they'd be days like
        this, they'd be days like this... Sure!
The Preacher said, every day's like this, every day's like
        this, every day's like this...   Bore!
Could the source of his moan
Be an emptiness- his own?
A man's reach should exceed his grasp, or what's a heaven,
        what's a heaven, what's a heaven.. For?!

Prophets

    The Prophets have no counterpart.
    They are unique in the spoken-written art.
    Their disciples recorded,
    Spoken words that they sorted,
    So they to us, the Word, may impart.

Acts

    It deals mostly with Saints Peter and Paul.
    Volume Two of Luke's Gospel recall.
    It's the Acts of God's Spirit,
    You can see it and hear it,
    A Wind that blows where it wills, over all.

Romans

    Our best guess is Paul wrote this last.
    His thinking seems studied, not fast.
    At times he's quite terse,
    With a great memory verse,
    The Good Wine last-served in this flask.

I Corinthians

    As a document for Christian selection
    Some see the Letter to Corinth, perfection.
    The opening features
    Arguments about preachers,
    And ends by taking up a collection.

Galatians   ...but faith working through love.   5:6
   Our best guess is Paul wrote this one fast.
   Send the word before the crisis is past.
   While the Law hangs us all,
   Grace lifts from The Fall.
   Faith made effective through Love, shall last.

2nd Peter and Jude   (2 Peter 3:7-8)
   Jude's warnings may once more be found,
   In 2nd Peter, where again they astound.
   There's a warning sublime:
   Watch for fire next time,
   And God's wristwatch is differently wound.

Revelation
   Author, John of Patmos, thought you would know,
   Isaiah, Daniel, Ezekiel, and so,
   He rewrote their old story
   In which God shines in glory,
   Wherefore John's readers found hope and not woe.

The Limerick Bible
   Like Dr. Suess who went "On Beyond Z".
   So the Spirit of God, don't you see,
   Just won't be fenced-in,
   By the limits of men,
   For who knows where next God will be?

A CONCLUDING BENEDICTION, the 100th, and final limerick:

Those with a liking for round numbers please read Psalm 100 and consider its placement under such an important round number. Could it stand as a banner over all the Psalms? Yes, and so...

Old 100th   Make a joyful noise to the Lord...

There are many things that we "know",
In our cerebral, intellectual flow.
But take that journey apart,
From the head, to the heart-
And may God grant "joyful noise" high and low.

...For the Lord is good; his steadfast love endures for ever, and his faithfulness to all generations.   Psalm 100:5